About the Author

Bill Wyman was born in London in 1936, and joined The Rolling Stones in 1962. Although best known for his music, Bill has pursued many other interests since leaving the stones in 1993. Bill is considered the unofficial archivist of the band; he is a prolific collector, photographer, and has kept diaries since a young age. He also has a great interest in history, archaeology and metal detecting.

Bill is a published author of twelve books including Stones From The Inside, Stone Alone, Wyman Shoots Chagall, Bill Wyman's Blues Odyssey and Rolling With The Stones.

Billy in the Wars

Bill Wyman

Billy in the Wars

Illustrated by Eoin Marron

Pegasus

PEGASUS PAPERBACK

© Copyright 2023
Ripple Productions

The right of Bill Wyman, Ripple Productions to be identified as author of
this work has been asserted by him in accordance with the
Copyright, Designs and Patents Act 1988

All Rights Reserved

No reproduction, copy or transmission of this publication
may be made without written permission.
No paragraph of this publication may be reproduced,
copied or transmitted save with the written permission of the
publisher, or in accordance with the provisions
of the Copyright Act 1956 (as amended).

Any person who does any unauthorised act in relation to
this publication may be liable to criminal
prosecution and civil claims for damage.

A CIP catalogue record for this title is
available from the British Library

ISBN-978-1-80468-020-9

Pegasus is an imprint of
Pegasus Elliot MacKenzie Publishers Ltd.
www.pegasuspublishers.com

First Published in 2023

Pegasus
Sheraton House Castle Park
Cambridge CB3 0AX England

Printed & Bound in Great Britain

To my grandmother Florence (French) Jeffery who had faith in me and taught me everything.

Acknowledgements

Thanks to my wife Suzanne Accosta Wyman for her help with the writing of this book, and to Ian Grenfell and Clementine de Banzie Lampard for their support.

Artwork by Eoin Marron.

Contents

Prologue 11

Beginnings 12

World War II 25

The Battle of Britain............................. 32

Evacuation.. 39

My Return to London......................... 51

Back With the Family 71

Doodle-Bug Alley 84

Happy Times with Gran Jeffery 93

The Family Return to London.......... 100

Peacetime 112

Epiloguc 1 120

Epilogue 2 123

Prologue

Throughout my early life and well into adulthood I was always cold and hungry. It wasn't until July 1964, when I was twenty-seven years old, and had been in The Rolling Stones for seven months, that we were able to move into a small flat over a garage in Penge High Street, that had central heating, a bathroom, hot water, and an inside toilet.

Courage is the theme of this story, as I witnessed the bravery of everybody around me during World War II and those hard times of my early childhood. I regret having not realised until now the courage of my parents, and I feel forever grateful to them for all they did for me as a child.

But it was my grandmother who gifted me the value of collecting and writing a diary that prepared me to be my stronger self. To fight against all odds, to take risks and be daring throughout my life. If it wasn't for her believing in me and teaching me the way out of my neighbourhood, I would not have plucked up enough courage to go against my friends', and my parents' wishes and quit my steady job to join a little blues band being formed called 'The Rollin' Stones'.

Beginnings

I am named after my father, William George Perks, who came from Lower Sydenham in South East London. He was born poor, I mean Charles Dickens poor, and had become since the age of fourteen a bricklayer by trade. On 16th of January 1935, he celebrated his twenty-first birthday by walking with his mate the three miles to the Penge Empire to see the Music Hall — the traditional variety concerts that were the most popular live entertainment at the time.

With the cheapest tickets in their hands, they climbed the stairs to the top of the house, only to find two very pretty girls sitting in their seats. Too shy and overcome with their beauty to ask them to move, they sat in the two empty seats directly next to the girls. During the interval they plucked up enough courage to converse with the girls and asked if they could walk them home after the show. Flattered by the boys' interest, the girls agreed. It turned out William and his mate both fancied Kathleen May Jeffery, known to her family and friends as Molly, so they tossed a coin to see who would be the one to walk her home. William called his favourite 'lucky tails', which he had called eight years earlier when captaining The Lewisham Schoolboy's cup-winning football team and earning him his one and only medal. He won, and later walked Molly the short distance to her home around the corner.

At Molly's doorstep they chatted, and as the sharp wind chilled them, William and Molly agreed to meet again soon, and their courtship began. Fate has always been present in my life, with events out of my control. I can't imagine what would have happened if Dad had called heads. The right toss seemed destined to happen.

Their meetings were unchaperoned, and they were restricted to public walks in the local lanes or romantically strolling by the little River Beck that meandered through Kelsey Park in Penge. Sometimes Dad would scrape together enough money to take Molly to the local cinema to see the latest romantic film. He was falling in love, and he invited her to his home to meet his family and friends. They were having an evening of 'sing-songs', where he played, having taught himself the piano and piano accordion when he was younger.

Six months after that first meeting, they were sitting on a park bench holding hands. I can well imagine my dad looking at his shoes, in his usual embarrassed way, and mumbling the words, "Will you marry me?" He didn't have money for an engagement ring, but Molly didn't care, and eagerly agreed, also fallen in love.

The following weekend William and Molly wanted to celebrate in style, and they went on a day's outing by train to Southend-on-Sea in Essex. After an enjoyable time together on the warm and sunny beach, they strolled along the sea front, window-shopping. There they came upon a small photographic studio, where they had their very first photo taken.

After she left school at the age of fourteen, my mother Molly had gone into domestic service for a family in Dulwich and was now happy to start a family of her own. My father, being the second oldest of ten children, had been contributing to his family's financial survival, together with helping to look after his younger brothers and sisters. But he had been saving a little money of his own as best he could, and he and Molly went together to a department store in Peckham, where they bought furniture for the tiny little flat that he had rented in Forest Hill in preparation for their wedding. The total cost was £75.12.0d, and William paid a deposit of £4.10.0d and agreed to pay ten shillings a week to pay it off. Molly was now eighteen, and dad was twenty-one.

With the coming of potential war in the background, they were married on his mother's birthday, Christmas Day 1935, at Christchurch, Penge, where Molly's family attended services, and where I would sing there as a choir boy years later. It was a small, quiet wedding, and being impoverished, there were no photos taken to celebrate their special day. I would realise in later years that mum become pregnant with me soon after, and exactly a year to the day of father tossing that coin at the Penge Empire.

Three months later they left their tiny flat in Forest Hill, and moved to 38 Miall Road, Lower Sydenham — further up the street from Dad's parents' house. There, my parents would often sit listening to the disturbing news of Germany's military build-up on Grandfather's handmade radio. It was possibly one of the only radios in our street, which consisted of ordinary terraced houses. They were all the same, three up and three down, with a small fenced-in front garden and a hedge. They had gas lighting, no bathroom, no electricity or heating or hot water, and the toilets were in the small back gardens attached to the rear of the houses.

In August 1936, Adolph Hitler opened the Olympic Games in Berlin, Germany, with the intention of glorifying the Aryan race and the Nazi regime. But Jesse Owens, the Black American track and field athlete became the star, winning four gold medals, and a furious Hitler stormed out of the stadium.

I was born two months later, just before midnight on Saturday 24th October 1936 at Lewisham Hospital. While there, mother caught scarlet fever and we were put into an isolation ward for a week. My father's visits consisted of standing below her window waving. Mum told me years later that he was very sad to be unable to spend time with his new wife and their first-born baby. She also told me that after we left the hospital, I was a problem baby. The neighbours complained so much about me crying, that my parents had to take turns walking me in the street at night in my pram until I fell asleep. This embarrassed Dad no end, as he was not happy to be seen doing what he regarded as 'women's work'.

When my grandmother Florence Jeffery (Mum's mother) came to the family gathering at our house to see the new-born baby for the first time, she picked me up in front of everyone and announced, "This child is going to be world-famous." Both my dad and everyone else there thought she was joking, and they all burst into laughter. It was unheard of in those days for a boy growing up in a working-class family to aspire to anything better than his parents.

In the highest part of London above Sydenham Hill at this time, stood the stunningly magnificent palace of glass called the Crystal Palace. It was originally built in 1851 for the Great Exhibition in Hyde Park, London. Queen Victoria's husband, Prince Albert, had it built to inspire the world with Britain's industrial achievements. When the original exhibition closed, the enormous glass and metal structure was relocated, and designed larger to impress. It brought life to our neighbourhood with unbelievable galleries of artefacts from all parts of the world, with extensive gardens and fountains. They would be later grassed over and converted into entertainment and sports facilities. The English F.A. Cup Finals were held there from 1895 to 1914, and the Crystal Palace football team was named after it when formed in 1905. They have been my favourite team since Dad took me to my first match after the war, on my tenth birthday in October 1946.

In the late evening of Monday 30th November 1936, when I was just five weeks old, my parents stood in the street holding me in their arms and experienced this magnificent glass building being destroyed by fire. They were mesmerised by the massive red glow that illuminated the south London sky for hours and hearing the wails of almost a hundred fire engines that came from all over London. They were unable to save it, and the magnificent Crystal Palace was burnt to the ground, never to rise again.

Throughout 1937 my parents were aware of the grave concerns across Britain, of Germany seen to be increasing their military build-up and holding the largest manoeuvres since the First World War.

In response, Britain and France began to increase their own military strength. Plans were also being made for the future evacuation on a voluntary basis for mothers and children to leave London and other major cities if war became imminent.

The threat of possible war with Germany increased when on 12th March 1938, they annexed Austria, and it was decreed by the British Government that air raid shelters should be erected in Britain's towns and cities. England had been manufacturing gas masks for some time, and began demonstrating them to the public, in fear of Germany possibly launching gas attacks, as they had done in the trenches in the First World War. By August that year the Royal Air Force was greatly strengthened when the legendary British Spitfire fighter plane entered service.

However, fears of war were put aside briefly, when on 30th September, Neville Chamberlain, the British prime minister, arrived home from meetings in Munich announcing to the cheering crowd and media that war had been averted. He was waving the agreement that Hitler had signed promising 'Peace in Our Time'.

A month later my brother Brian John was born but was always known as John. I was told by Mum that

I had been a very early walker and talker — as she put it. But John was frailer than me, and Mother took a great shine to him, seeming to be much more attentive to his needs than mine. She expected me to just get on with it, which I did in the end, resulting in me becoming much more independent that he would ever be.

In February 1939, Anderson air raid shelters, made with corrugated metal, were being installed as planned in most back gardens. They were partly covered by a foot of soil for more protection. Then gas masks were issued to everyone. The smaller children's masks were made to resemble Walt Disney's Mickey Mouse in an attempt to make them less daunting. The older children had more grown-up ones and were obliged to carry them wherever they went, in brown leather boxes with shoulder straps. I remember Mum later showing me how to put a gas mask on over my face, causing me to feel very claustrophobic, and scared and worried that I wouldn't be able to breathe with it on.

Meanwhile, Germany had completed its occupation of Czechoslovakia, and signed a military alliance with Italy, which increased the possibility of war. Britain and France pledged to defend Poland against any attacks by Germany, and the Territorial Army was doubled, and Britain began to seriously brace itself for war.

In late August, Blackout Regulations were imposed by the government. This required the public to put tape across the window glass, and then to cover all of the windows and doors with whatever materials they could find. This was done to stop the house lights being seen and benefitting the German planes if they attacked our towns. Throughout my early childhood I would live with these blacked out windows, being unable to look out into our street, and being scared of the total darkness it caused in the house at night. A fear that has stayed with me into my adult life.

Street lighting was also extinguished, and vehicles were required to drive on their dimmed side lights, making driving much more difficult. However, England was blessed by the invention of what was called 'cats eyes' by the Yorkshire inventor and businessman Percy Shaw. They were made of flexible rubber and could be driven over without a problem. They contained two marbles that would reflect any small light, making it possible for drivers to follow the centre of the darkened roads in safety. The downside was that when us children got a little older, we began to damage these, having discovered that we could dig out the marbles to play with.

It was then advised that mothers and children should start to think about possible evacuation from the cities. But families were confused and concerned about being separated from their loved ones. I imagined my parents would have had many conversations with friends and relatives looking for guidance. They finally decided that we could not evacuate at that moment in time. Because of my mother's pregnancy, and with two small children under the age of three in tow, relocation was physically out of the question.

World War II

On 1st September 1939, Germany, under the control of Adolf Hitler, invaded Poland by land and air. World War II commenced two days later, when Britain and France declared war on Germany for breaking their earlier agreement. A month later the British Expeditionary Force of almost 160,000 soldiers left for France.

On a cold day in early December, I was frightened to see a doctor arrive to visit my mum who was 'ill' in bed. He carried with him a big black bag, and when he left after seeing Mother, I had a baby sister. I was told by Dad that the doctor had brought my sister in his bag. She was named Anne Rosemary, and being the first daughter, she became my father's favourite.

It began to snow and went on freezing throughout the rest of the month, but I was a happy three-year-old, with my first gift at Christmas. It was a small wind-up coloured metal bi-plane that ran along the ground and looped-the-loop. After Christmas the weather worsened, and we were very cold in the house. It continued to snow, and it was reported on Grandad's radio that the Thames had frozen for the first time since 1888, and the worst storms of the century were sweeping England.

German U-boats (submarines) were now attacking and sinking merchant ships bringing foodstuffs to England. As a result of this, food rationing began. People were allocated small portions of pretty much everything, with the government being forced to tell the public what they were and weren't allowed to eat.

With the birth of my sister, and the imminent threat of air raids on London, my mother, now just twenty-two-years-old made the heart-breaking decision to leave London with us three young infants. We left home and were evacuated to the safety of Pembrokeshire in Wales. My dad stayed in London as he needed to continue to work. I, aged three and not understanding the seriousness of the situation, found this new adventure exciting, travelling on my first train. When we arrived, we settled into a little rural village in lovely quiet countryside. I loved the companionship of nature and the sense of calm that only spending hours in the fresh air can bring. I have faint memories of playing in a grassy country lane, chasing butterflies, and spending my days enjoying the open countryside, instead of sitting on a curb looking at tarmac or flagstones bordering the gutter. This opened a window in my mind to the beauties of nature.

However, Mother was not happy, and this window closed for me when after a few weeks we returned to London. With no big bombing raids in Britain in those first few months of the war (then known as the Phoney War), many evacuees returned home. On the way to the railway station my mother gave us our very first bananas. God knows where she got them from. We'd never had bananas before, and we hungrily ate them in seconds. Still hungry and wanting more, we tried to eat the peeled skins, and everything came up as just as fast as it had gone down. Mum was far from pleased, and I passed a silent journey home, staring out of the carriage window, watching as the countryside flashed by.

A short time later while playing with a torch bulb I accidentally swallowed it. My mother, worrying that it might have broken inside me, rushed me to the South London Children's Hospital around the corner. There the doctor persuaded me to eat a sandwich filled with wads of cotton wool between bread slices. It's almost impossible to explain the awful feeling of trying to bite into the dryness of it. Pulling it apart with my teeth, gave me a horrible feeling like fingernails on a blackboard, and then chewing it and having to swallow was really traumatic. Needless to say, these sensations I experienced were never forgotten, and I have had a revulsion of touching cotton wool ever since.

While there the doctor noticed the large white patches on my skin that were all over my body. Apparently, I'd had them since I was a baby. He diagnosed them as being a harmless allergy to wool, which was a funny thing, considering that he'd just made me swallow a cotton wool sandwich! My mum never took on board my allergy to wool, probably because new clothes were too much of a luxury. I continued to have the patches until my teenage years by which time they had disappeared. I remember how uncomfortable I always was, and itchy clothing still gives me the horrors.

That April, Germany invaded Denmark and Norway, and it was soon reported that Holland and Belgium had both surrendered to Germany. Meanwhile here in England Winston Churchill, who was to become my future hero, had taken over the reins of prime minister, and had immediately formed a coalition government.

A few days later, as France capitulated, I recall the shocked family members meeting up at Dad's parents' house down the road to listen to the news crackling through Grandad's home-made radio, of the courageous evacuation of the British Expeditionary Force from the beaches of Dunkirk. Many thousands of troops were being rescued by a huge fleet of destroyers, ferry boats, fishing boats, and any other small boat that could make the journey. This is one of my first memories of my family talking proudly of England's involvement in the war. Even at my very early age, I was feeling pride for my country.

Things were still relatively peaceful in London, and the weather had improved from the cold dark wintery days to fresh sunny spring mornings. Dad was by now doing private work locally, and on the weekends, he would take me to work with him, sitting on the crossbar of his bicycle. While he was laying bricks and mixing cement, he kept me happy busily moving sand backwards and forwards from one pile to another with my little wooden spade and trolley that he'd bought me. He was probably doing it to give Mum a break, but it's a memory I hold dear. He was probably just showing off his three-year-old son to his workmates.

That month I recall my Aunt Bessie, Dad's youngest sister who was ten, taking me to visit my great grandmother, the mother of my Gran Perks. Her name was Charlotte Roberts (née Rulton), and she lived a short walk away in Forest Hill. Her house seemed huge to me, and I loved her back garden that was filled with fruit trees in blossom and had a magical carpet of bluebells and daffodils, that I happily ran through. As we were leaving, she pressed a shiny silver sixpence into my hand, which in today's money would be more like a pound — a lot of money for a three-year-old boy back then. This was the first and last time I ever saw her. I enquired about her years later and was told that she had died when the house was destroyed during a bombing raid in 1944.

That June, Italy declared war on Britain, and with France having now become a fascist state, and Germany having occupied the Channel Islands of Jersey and Guernsey, Churchill reported that Britain would now fight alone. Four of Dad's younger brothers had been called up by now for military service, and his eldest sister Alice had joined the Women's Auxiliary Air Force. I felt very proud, seeing my young uncles arriving and leaving my grandparents' house in their smart military uniforms. Two in the army, one in the air force, and the youngest in the navy. My family was covering sea, land and air, as Winston Churchill stated at the time.

The Battle of Britain

The Battle of Britain began on 10th July 1940, and we soon got used to the Germans flying over without bombing us in south London. They were more concerned with attacking the City and the London docks. I remember hearing a heavy droning sound like thunder that brought everyone out into the street, knowing they were not in direct danger. Standing with my parents and the neighbours, looking up high, I saw the sky completely filled with formations of hundreds of German bombers passing over. The whole street cheered in unison at the sight of the white trails of our Spitfires and Hurricanes attacking them.

It wasn't until the Germans wanted to wear down our morale that they started to bomb the London suburbs. I was either too young to remember, or I wasn't aware of the fear that everyone around me was feeling when the war arrived on our doorsteps. Massive daylight raids of over 1,000 German planes were being sent over to bomb Britain each day. The blitz of London continued with Hitler swearing to reduce London to rubble. We were obliged to spend most days and nights in the air raid shelters in our gardens. With my uniformed uncles coming and going all the time, I would sometimes sleep with my grandparents' family in their shelter down the street, sharing the mattress that tightly fitted the six-foot earthen floor, and thus easing the strain on Mum and Dad.

The neighbourhood was a war zone, with the sight of barrage balloons hanging in the sky everywhere, anti-aircraft guns and searchlights in every park area with men behind sandbanks in the bunkers, and the sound of the pom-pom guns on the back of trucks tearing up and down the streets firing shells at the German planes overhead. When the air raids were over, Grandad Perks would take me out in the street where he would pick up shrapnel for his collection and add them to the massive piece in his cupboard under the stairs.

I recall Grandma Perks always having a cigarette in her mouth, lighting a new one from the remains of the last. I was comfortable with her, but frightened of Grandfather, who was always a little grumpy with me. He'd fought in the First World War and had lost his right eye fighting as a machine gunner in Salonica in Greece. He returned to civilian life with just an empty socket which always scared me. When I had to return to our house, I didn't like to kiss him goodbye, because of his bristly moustache. I would rush out the front door to avoid him.

As a youngster Grandfather had been a bare-fist fighter, and he was tough. His best friend in those days was the South of England bare-fist boxing champion Edgar Beard. I recall seeing Grandad's hand-painted photo of them together that hung in their front room. Grandad had a hobby of breeding racing pigeons, and he'd built a large aviary in the small back garden. He must have had fifty or sixty birds, which he raced. He was a popular man locally, having bred many champion birds over the years that won him prizes. The passage that led from the front door of the house was adorned with original oil paintings of these famous winners. All of his earnings seemed to go on this hobby, and the only benefits the ten children got were the little pigeon eggs for breakfast or tea.

He spent most evenings at The Bell Pub at Bell Green at the bottom of the road, for a pint of beer and his tobacco, which he rolled his cigarettes from. Sometimes he would send one of his children to the off licence to collect his beer. He was a bit of a tyrant at home, and my dad and his nine siblings suffered because of it. They were always heavily punished for even the smallest offences. On many occasions, Dad was obliged to get up in the early mornings and push a wheelbarrow to a London railway station. There he would deliver a hamper of his father's pigeons to travel north to race. Dad would walk back home, and be late for school and often get the cane.

Father would always say that us children had it so much better than he did as a child and would tell us what it was like for him. He talked of arriving home late from school, or have scuffed his shoes, and Grandad would give him 'a thick ear'. His father would sometimes smack him for no reason, and when Dad would enquire what it was for, Grandad would say, "That's for nothing. Just wait till you do something."

But Grandad did have a soft side. He was a great lover of the music hall, and on Saturday evenings, in the gas-lit kitchen, where he would settle down with his beer and cigarettes, he would demand that the children take it in turns to dress up. Then, commencing with the youngest, they would be expected to stand on the kitchen table, and sing songs imitating the likes of the great music hall stars of the time, like Harry Champion, Marie Lloyd and George Robey. As soon as they had completed their individual acts, accompanied by laughter, cheers or boos, they were whisked upstairs to bed, often with a gentle slap around the legs with his belt.

There was a brief lull in the bombing, as Germany changed its targets to other major cities in England, with Coventry being the worst hit. Then after Christmas Germany again attempted to set fire to the city of London, with massive bombing raids causing fires to rage out of control. Many of the public who had no access to air raid shelters in central London, were now sheltering and basically living in the underground stations.

In May 1941, London was subjected to a final onslaught of almost 600 bombers who rained bombs and incendiaries on London, and the loss of life was at its worst. We were forced to spend most nights and sometimes days in our damp, musky, air raid shelter. There was sweet revenge when we heard that the British navy had sunk the finest German battleship, the *Bismarck*, in the Atlantic.

A few weeks later the Battle of Britain was pretty much over, thanks to our marvellous young pilots who had held the German Air Force at bay. But we were still suffering from the occasional raids that happened during the following days and nights.

One day at work Dad broke for lunch with one of his mates and they went to a local café. Suddenly sirens went off and they rushed out, running for shelter as bombs began to fall. Dad ducked behind the closest thing he saw which was a chicken-wire fence, while his mate ran down the street, where Dad saw him get hit by an incendiary bomb. Right before his eyes he watched his friend burn to death.

These traumatic moments would stay with Dad for life. He would talk about them in his very matter-of-fact way, showing no emotion, and I never saw him cry.

Germany, having by now failed to bring Britain to her knees, turned and focussed its attention on the invasion of Russia. There were still a few air raids, but we were now able to sleep peacefully in our beds most nights, although our comfort was short lived.

Evacuation

Evacuations changed lives, separated families and destroyed relationships. Dad by now felt that London was too dangerous a place for his family, with his fundamental duty to protect them being out of his control. So, in early July 1941 he made the monumental decision to move the family into a safer environment. The Women's Voluntary Service and the local council under the government's evacuation scheme, were encouraging mothers to evacuate with their children if they were under the age of five, and they were able to give some help to Mum and Dad.

Mother and us kids left our home in Sydenham, leaving Dad to work on alone. We travelled by train to Victoria Station, and on to Euston Station, where we journeyed the one hundred and thirty miles north to Nottingham. We travelled on to Mansfield Woodhouse, fifteen miles north of Nottingham itself. There we settled into the home of a 'host' family called Crowder, who lived in Sherwood Street, and had kindly agreed to give us temporary accommodation.

Old Mrs Crowder was stone deaf, but an expert lipreader, and ruled her family with a firm hand, but she was always very sweet and motherly to us. She had a very meek husband called Tom, with four sons and two daughters: Ray, Cyril, Harold, Desmond, Joyce and Maisy. It was a full and busy household. They made us feel at home immediately, and we all became very close. The house always smelled of the wonderful homemade bread that I watched and helped Mrs Crowder make, and thinking of it still makes my mouth water.

When mother discovered that Cyril was working as a builder repairing hangars on the local airfields as part as the war effort, she managed to get him to secure a job for Dad. Mrs Crowder was kind enough to agree to have him join us, and the Crowders' house became even more crowded.

Between the back of the Sherwood Street and the Coke Street houses, was a shared open communal backyard, where the washing lines hung, wheelbarrows were stored, and the odd bicycle could be seen. We would play games in the dirt, collecting small pieces of broken blue and white pottery that we found all over the yard. Brother John and I were made friendly fun of by the local kids and mothers because of our Cockney accents. We would ask Mum for bread and butter (which we called 'bread and buppy' back in London), and we were christened 'the Buppy Kids', which we regarded as a very amusing nickname.

One day Bubbles (Harold) and Diddy (Desmond) Crowder took me by bus to Mansfield on market day, where the bustle and noises were fresh and exciting. They bought me a little notebook and a small pencil, which I treasured. Another day they took me to the wide, but shallow, River Maun, just over four miles away, where we spent the day wading in the clear water, fishing with our little fishing nets for minnows and sticklebacks, which we brought home in jam-jars.

I loved this river, with its clear shallow water over the soft pebbly bottom, and one day when the boys wouldn't take me again, I decided to go alone. God knows how I found my way there, not yet five years old, but I actually walked the four miles there and back. I spent the day paddling in the warm water fishing, and a giant fish, obviously a trout, swam through my bare legs. I was mesmerised by it, never having seen a fish so large. However, when I returned home at dusk, Mother was furious, not knowing where I had been all day, and I got a smack and was sent off to bed. Nobody seemed interested in my wonderful sighting of the giant fish, which for me made it all worthwhile.

Throughout the July summer break, mothers and children were employed to go pea-picking at the local farms. We shared small huts with earthen floors to rest from the sun and eat our sandwiches. Us children would eat almost as many peas as we picked, and consequently suffered painful tummy aches, but we still loved the fresh sweet taste of them.

The holidays ended in early September, and I began to attend the York Street School, which was almost a mile away. To get there I would walk with my school friends to the edge of town, then on through country lanes that by-passed farms and fields. The countryside was wonderful to a little city boy, seeing the horses, cows and sheep grazing peacefully for the first time. The expeditions into the lanes and fields, finding lizards, toads and birds' nests, are still some of my fondest memories during those strife-torn days.

One day on the way home I managed to catch a cute little toad, and on arrival I got a small cardboard box from Mrs Crowder to put my toad in, together with a little grass and cabbage. I put it in the coal shed attached to the rear of the house, but by the next morning he had escaped. I searched for him for days, but he was gone forever.

Other times my friends and I would go down to the railway embankment at the bottom of Sherwood Street and cut branches from the large bushes that grew there and make bows and arrows. We would also visit a little metal turning factory nearby, where we'd collect the oily steel shavings, shaped like springs, and play unremembered games with them. During these brief times everything was an adventure.

I also recall playing regularly around the old coal tips at the Sherwood Colliery just out of town, where vegetation was beginning to grow. We would be thrilled to see the occasional mole there.

We had been warned by our friends that some local bullies hung out around there, called 'Smasher Smedley and his Gang', but we were very fortunate that they never crossed paths with us.

We would sit and watch the buckets of coal waste travel along the high wires and empty their loads, forming new tips, and then return to be refilled again. When in 1971, I saw the Michael Caine film *Get Carter*, it featured almost identical scenes, although these were filmed at a Newcastle coalmine.

Once brother John and I were playing around between two old coal tips. Water had settled into a thick black swamp, and a car could be seen in the middle, upright and half-submerged. My sister Anne, not yet two, left her pushchair and stepped into the sludge and couldn't escape. We dragged her free, leaving one of her shoes to vanish into the murky depths. We put her back into her pushchair and took her home crying.

Shortly after that our family were able to settle into a little house that had become vacant across the yard from the Crowder house in Coke Street. It was there that I spent my fifth birthday. Yet even in rural Nottinghamshire the war was never far away. One night I was woken by the sound of a plane crashing nearby, and the whole room lit up with an eerie red glow. This immediately took me back to the fear of the bombing I thought we left behind in London. Next day we heard that the German pilot had bailed out safely and was captured by the local military, and that the local ladies had taken possession of his parachute and had cut it up to make clothing and other necessities.

A month later the British offensive was launched in the Western Desert, with my Uncle Jack, Mum's youngest brother, serving with the Eighth Army on the anti-aircraft guns. Father, now twenty-seven, was called up to do his military service. He had a medical examination in Mansfield, where he passed Grade II, due to poor eyesight. He was kitted out, and did his combat and trade training as a mechanic.

On 7th December 1941, the Japanese Air Force attacked Pearl Harbour, destroying most of the American Pacific fleet. This brought America into the war, and Britain and America declared war on Japan.

January 1942 began with huge snowfalls, the likes of which I had never seen before or since. It snowed throughout the days and nights and by morning we were all completely snowed in. We couldn't open our back doors until the menfolk dug us out, and they then created deep trenched passageways through the five feet high snow between the houses. I clearly remember being able to walk through the snowy passageway over to the Crowder house where I wanted the boys to come out and play with me, but that was impossible with the snow so deep.

Most of the snow had cleared a few days later, but it was still very icy everywhere. I walked down towards the railway station at the bottom of Sherwood Street by myself, where there was a large sloping open area near the metal turning factory. There I stood watching the fathers and older children playing on tremendously long slides, while others skated down the slopes on their home-made sledges. I felt sad being unable to join in with everyone as I had no sledge of my own, and I just stood alone watching the fun, feeling rather left out.

By the end of March, the RAF were able to retaliate against the German bombing raids, with their own terror bombing campaigns against ports, industrial areas and military targets in both occupied France and Germany. Then the following month after their great success, Hitler insisted on the smaller towns in England being razed to the ground with further bombing raids.

I was by now starting to notice that Mum was acting very nervously and would often lose her patience with us. She would tell me I was 'getting in her hair' and would insist on me going out to play. I was very happy to obey her wishes, as I loved being in the open air playing with my friends as that early spring arrived.

The happiness I felt was however being clouded by the bad times I was having at school. My young lady teacher would ridicule my Cockney accent in front of the class and insist that I talked in the local dialect. She would smack me when I didn't, and I began to play truant to avoid her, together with a few other boys who were also unhappy at school. We would leave home in the mornings and meet up at our secret hideaway in the old church ruin on the outskirts of the town. There we would sit around the little bonfires we made to keep warm. I was by now bright enough to pocket the occasional box of matches from home for these escapades.

After returning to school on the odd occasion it was the same problem with the beastly teacher, and I continued to play truant whenever I could. I was desperately looking forward to the arrival of the summer holidays to escape from school.

Mother finally discovered before the end of term that I had been playing truant and was beside herself with anger and disappointment. I remember returning home one afternoon thinking I'd been so clever pretending to have been at school. But, when I open the door I was confronted by my father, who had been given a weekend pass, and had returned home from the army base. He was standing over my mum who was crying in the chair. She was telling him that she just couldn't cope with us three small children any more, being seven months pregnant, and now having discovered that I was playing truant from school. This was about all she could bear, and she was showing me no sympathy about my teacher's brutality. That evening they talked at length about the problems, and finally agreed to make arrangements for me to return to live with my Grandmother Jeffery and her family back in Penge, to ease the strain on Mum. They wrote to Grandma a few days later and she immediately replied and happily agreed to take on their unruly little five-year-old.

Mum and Dad sat me down and talked to me about their plans. I was so happy about not having to go to school again and face my horrible teacher, but very confused and unsure about leaving the family. I'd visited my gran on a number of occasions with Mum before we left for Nottingham, and she was always very sweet and nice with me. I went off to bed, and quietly lying there I thought about joining Gran back in London. I began to get very excited about this new adventure, but I was wondering how I was going to get there.

My Return to London

After the weekend Dad returned to camp, and that morning Mum got me dressed, packed a few of my belongings in a small bag with a jam sandwich, and we left home with my gas mask over my shoulder. We travelled by bus to Mansfield, and on to Nottingham's main railway station, with me beginning to feel a little worried. After buying my train ticket, Mum took me to the waiting train, and my worries worsened. She put me into a carriage that I shared with an old lady who was also on her way to London. Mum asked her to please keep an eye on me, and she kissed me goodbye and tearfully left.

During that two-and-a-half-hour train journey, I sat looking out of the window and watching the changing scenery skim past. I began to think sadly of my family and the friends I would miss, and the lovely countryside I had enjoyed during my year of evacuation. I ate my jam sandwich and the nice lady sharing the carriage gave me a little drink of the tea in her thermos bottle. We chatted throughout the rest of the trip which cheered me up.

We arrived in London and when I left the train with the nice lady, I saw my Grandmother Jeffery waiting on the platform. I said goodbye to the lady and ran to Gran, who welcomed me warmly, giving me a big hug. From there we took the bus to Victoria Station and travelled the short twenty-minute journey to Penge East Station. We left the train, and carrying my little bag and gas mask, she walked me to her home at 36 Blenheim Road — one of the slummiest streets in Penge.

I soon discovered that Grandma, who was fifty-seven years old at the time, was very knowledgeable on a number of subjects, being an avid reader of rented library books. She was a wonderful, sweet and kindly lady, who gave me the love and attention I craved. I immediately felt at home in their little flat that she shared with my grandfather, Herbert Henry Jeffery, my Aunt Dorothy, and Nobby Everett, a lodger and family friend.

Grandma's maiden name was French, and before her marriage she lived in Beckenham, Kent. After leaving school in 1898 at the age of fourteen, she went into service as a housemaid for a family in Wells Park Road, Upper Sydenham. After working there for two years, the great cricketer W.G. Grace retired after playing his last test match for England in June 1899. By chance he moved into the house next door to where she worked. She later told me that as she was leaving one afternoon, he was in his front garden, and pleasantly gave her 'the time of day'. Although he looked rather scary with his huge beard, it did encourage her to become very fond of the game, which would continue throughout the rest of her life. When I was living with her in my early teens, we would sit together in their new house in Garden Road, Anerley, and watch the cricket on her little six-inch black and white television set, where the players were often just little dots on the tiny screen.

I learned from her that grandfather, now sixty-one, had been very clever in his youth, and in those early days he would journey on horseback from Penge to Beckenham across the fields to visit her at her family home. They married in 1909 and had seven children, but he was disabled after an accident at work in 1917, when he was thirty-six years old. He was apparently in a coma for weeks, and after finally recovering, had to be re-taught everything, and never returned to his former self. This must have thrown a huge burden on Grandma, throughout those child-bearing years. However, I would soon discover that she was a strong woman who could adapt herself to any situation.

Grandfather, who had all of the necessary tools for the job, earned money masterfully repairing boots and shoes. He had been a butcher by trade before the accident, and would also earn money expertly slaughtering chickens, ducks and rabbits, for our neighbours. I would sit fascinated watching him as he brought them clucking or quacking into the scullery, and would then wring their necks, and kill the rabbits with a strike behind the head. I helped him put the dead fowls in hot water and then pluck them, before he cut them open and gutted them. Once he opened up a chicken and took out a whole string of eggs, going from almost full-size, all the way down to ones like tiny peas, and he lined them up in a row on the kitchen table for me to wonder over. I never felt any horror seeing him butcher them, and I was fully aware of his pride in showing off his many skills to me.

Their lodger was Nobby Everett, who worked in the council yard at the top of the street and was always nice and friendly to me. He'd also had an accident at work years earlier, where large paving stones had fallen on him, permanently damaging his right arm. He had bolts through the elbow and wrist and always stood holding his arm, taking the weight with his other hand. He would help the family financially.

My Aunt Dorothy, mum's youngest sister, was seventeen-years-old at that time, and worked at the Admiralty in London. She would bring home pencils and sheets of note paper for Grandma to use, and Gran would give me some to keep me occupied. I would sit for hours writing column after column of numbers. I never knew why, but numbers always fascinated me, and still do to this day. It probably explains why maths was my best subject at school and would later contribute to my love of archiving and documenting everything.

Their flat was entered from the downstairs staircase and was on the first floor of the house. It consisted of two bedrooms, a kitchen and scullery. The toilet was, as was usually the case, located in the garden attached to the back of the house. It was naturally shared with the people living downstairs. It contained pieces of torn newspaper on a large metal hook. To avoid having to go out there at night, everyone used chamber pots that were kept under their beds, and Gran had the distasteful job of emptying and cleaning them out each morning.

As was the case in every house I'd ever lived in up to this time, there was no electricity, and the rooms were gas-lit. The only heating came from the kitchen stove, which Grandma kept immaculately clean and polished, with black lead. We had no bathroom, and everybody washed in a bowl in the scullery sink, in water that was heated in a kettle. We cleaned our teeth with smoker's tooth powder and what was called tooth-soap, but I don't recall having a toothbrush, and would just use my fingers.

The rooms were always a little clouded with smoke from Grandfather's and Nobby's cigarettes, which was regarded as normal in those days. Most everybody smoked in their homes and it was widely advertised in magazines and newspapers, and glamourised on the radio and in the films of the day. It was regarded as a morale booster during the war and serving soldiers were supplied with a free cigarette or tobacco ration. Nobody regarded smoking as a danger to health, although I was aware that the smoke caused Gran to have regular coughing fits, which always worried me.

On Saturday evenings, water was heated in the copper (where Gran washed our dirty clothes) and in saucepans on the gas stove. Then Gran would take down the zinc bath that hung on the back of the scullery door and fill it. She would bathe me first, and wash my hair, and I would be put to bed, while the adults would then take turns to bathe individually and privately.

Grandma and Aunt Dorothy had individual single beds in the small middle room, while Grandad, Nobby and I slept in our own beds in the larger front room. I often recall being woken up at night in my little camp bed by the two semi invalids across the room, who would be snoring their heads off.

Our bedroom contained a huge Victorian sideboard that was full of little ornaments and artefacts that

Grandma had collected over the years. As I had no toys, Grandma gave me a little china house from these and a set of seven little white ivory elephants that got smaller and smaller. When I was tucked up warmly in my little bed, she would sit beside me and recite many stories and rhymes, including *The Little Crooked House* and *The House That Jack*

Built, until I fell asleep peacefully, with my little house under my pillow. The ownership of these little objects meant the world to me at the time and I treasured them.

The Crooked Man nursery rhyme went as follows:

There was a crooked man, who walked a crooked mile
He found a crooked sixpence against a crooked stile
He bought a crooked cat that caught a crooked mouse
And they all lived together in a little crooked house

The last verse of the nursery rhyme for *The House That Jack Built* was as follows:

This is the farmer sowing the corn,
That kept the cock that crowed in the morn.
That woke the priest all shaven and shorn,
That married the man all tattered and torn,
That kissed the maiden all forlorn,
That milked the cow with the crumpled horn,
That tossed the dog,
That worried the cat,
That killed the rat,
That ate the malt
That lay in the house that Jack built.

On the wall above Grandad's bed was a faded photo, that looked more like a drawing to me. It was a picture of Gran's first child, and my mother's eldest sister, Florence Grace (Holly), who had fallen in the school playground in 1915 at the age of five. She had complained of bad headaches for a few days, and finally died from a brain haemorrhage. Every Christmas Grandma would put a sprig of holly over the photo, and members of the family would always say that they saw a tear on her cheek at that time. I must say that I kept a constant watch on the picture, but never saw any tears — but she always looked such an angelic and beautiful five-year-old. I would stare at it and always wondered why her life had been so sadly cut short.

The air raid shelter in the back garden was shared by a few families, and the air raids and bombing were still going on intermittently. By now we had a huge bomb site between the bottom of the road and the High Street where houses and shops had been demolished. There was another flattened area at the top of the road on our side, where vegetation was starting to grow. Then across the road at the top were the shells of two houses still standing, where we would sometimes play.

On the air raid shelter's earthen top and in the surrounding garden, Grandma grew runner beans, peas, lettuce, mint, and a few herbs, intermingled with her favourite flowers, sweet peas and pansies. I loved helping her in that little garden, and especially liked the smell of the mint, which she sometimes made into sauce for Sunday dinner. Helping her in the garden eased my longing for my family and the countryside I'd left behind in Nottingham. I was more than happy in this loving home that I shared with Grandma, who would always come up with things to feed my curiosity and imagination and keep me out of trouble.

On 1st September 1942, Grandma took me to the small photographic studio round the corner in Maple Road, where I had my photo taken, wearing new shorts and a little white blouse. Back home Gran sat me down and I wrote 'To dear Mummy from Billy' on the back. It was a gift Gran had arranged for Mum, and is the earliest photo of me in existence, and my earliest writing. Gran posted it off to Mum next day for her twenty-fifth birthday.

Most afternoons during that summer holiday Gran would sit me down and start to go through the basics of improving my reading, writing and my maths. I loved the way she taught, inspiring me with new ideas and knowledge on a variety of subjects. She also taught me how to recite the alphabet backwards — which was just a simple rhyme that went as follows — ZYX — W — V — UTS — RQP — ONM and LKJ — IHGF — EDCBA.

A week later school commenced after the holiday break, and Gran walked me to the Melvin Infants School, where I was to continue my education. Mum and her brothers and sisters had all earlier attended school there. I was very unsure and nervous on the way, wondering if the teachers would be hitting me again, and if I would have to play truant if I didn't like it. However, my fears were soon forgotten, as I felt far happier here than at school in Nottingham. The teachers were very nice, and I made lots of friends. I was supplied with a new standard gas mask in a brown leather box with a shoulder strap and was instructed to carry it with me wherever I went.

The teacher took our names and later asked if anyone knew the alphabet. I replied that I knew it backwards, which seemed to stun her. I stood up and casually recited to the class the simple rhyme that Gran had taught me. I sat back down at my desk, impressing everyone, and having my first moment of glory. Telling Gran back home at lunchtime of my achievement, she gave me that big understanding smile that always warmed my heart. For my first few days, Gran walked me to school each morning, and met me at lunchtime to eat my small dinner, and then walk me back. She'd return to pick me up at the end of the day and we'd return home. She would then question me on what I had learned that day.

Throughout my childhood the lunchtime meal was dinner, and because of the rationing Gran made us cheap meals that were filling. The evening meal was referred to as teatime, where mostly bread was eaten with a variety of spreads. We had fish or meat pastes in small jars, or jam and dripping on bread. Grandma also made rock cakes, sponges, and fantastic bread puddings with crispy crusts that I loved.

On 20th October 1942, my second sister, Judith Cecelia Grace, was born in Mansfield Woodhouse, Nottingham, and four days later I enjoyed my sixth birthday. I was presented with a little wooden whip and spinning top that Grandfather had made for me, and I happily played with it in the street. I also learned a multitude of street games and rhymes from my friends, that were recited as we played with skipping ropes and tennis balls. The street was safe at this time with no transport whatsoever apart from the milkman and the cart he pulled by hand. We also played on the bomb sites in our road, and on the other bomb sites on way home from school.

We were spending very few days and nights in the air raid shelters, as the bombing had been reduced to the occasional air raid by a few odd planes. The evenings were relatively peaceful, and a regular happening would be Gran, Grandad and Nobby walking me to the Lord Palmerston pub in Maple Road. There they would sit me outside with a few other kids, with a glass of lemonade and an arrowroot biscuit, while they would be inside enjoying their drinks with games of darts, shove ha'penny and dominoes. I would peep in the door, when people went in and out, curious to see what was going on in that warm, noisy and friendly place.

A month later, my father reported to Matlock Baths, Derbyshire, and while there, he carved me a small unpainted wooden airplane, which he sent to Grandma's house for my Christmas present. It was the first gift he ever gave me, and it made me realise that he must be missing me, as I was missing him, which brought a tear to my eye.

The number one record that winter was Bing Crosby's *White Christmas*, from the film *Holiday Inn*, which became one of the biggest-selling single records of all time. The family had by now acquired a radio from somewhere, and the song was the first music I can remember that inspired me. Doubly so because of Gran singing it to me at bedtime in that cosy home that I loved so dearly.

In early January 1943, Father was posted near to Chiswick, London, where he passed his driving course, and was then posted on to the No 23 (Training) Group RAF in Norwich, Norfolk, where he successfully passed the mechanics course, and joined the REME (Royal Electrical Mechanical Engineers). He never came to visit me while he was there, although he was not that far away.

A week later British planes began to bomb Berlin, and Hitler retaliated with renewed heavy bombing attacks on London. The sirens would wail, and we would jump out of our beds and rush to the shelter in the back garden. On the way there we would see the dozens of searchlights criss-crossing each other, scouring the sky for the approaching enemy planes. These huge lights were positioned with the anti-aircraft guns in bunkers in all of our local parks. Safe in the shelter the candles would be lit, and I would cuddle up to Gran to keep warm in that freezing cold shelter.

There was a handsome man called Tom whose family were friends with Gran and lived a few doors away. Tom was a soldier, and when he returned home on weekend passes. I would run to him as he walked down the street and he'd give me a friendly hug. He was very fatherly towards me and I loved to see him in his uniform and spend a little time with him. He sometimes brought us a few oranges, which were very rare at the time. I always called him my Uncle Tom, and he became the role model for my dad at the time

On most days when we left school, we would walk down Melvin Road, turn into Maple Road, and on the corner of the next street, Padua Road, there was a large pub called The London Tavern. We would walk round to the pub's back garden and look through the knotholes in the fence at the fascinating sight of about half-a-dozen small monkeys playing in a large cage on the far wall of the pub's garden. This was an amazing sight, as I'd never seen monkeys before, having never been to a zoo, and we all revelled in watching their amusing capers and cries.

At lunchtime on Wednesday 20th January 1943, while we were again watching the monkeys play, the air raid sirens went off, and we all quickly dispersed. My friend Derek Stuttley and I ran down Maple Road towards our respective homes. But by the time we turned into the top of Blenheim Road, we saw a German fighter-bomber, that we later learned was a Messerschmitt, appear at the bottom of the road and begin to roar up the street towards us just above the rooftops. It was firing its guns, and we ran to the only cover there was, ducking behind the small coping-wall of the first house, as it roared over our heads past us.

We jumped up and quickly ran to our homes further down the road, with my heart pumping rapidly in my chest and gasping for breath. On arrival I rushed upstairs into the flat, where Gran was anxiously waiting for me. She grabbed me in her welcoming arms, and we hurried down the back staircase, to get to the safety of the air raid shelter in the garden. The staircase had a large skylight window, and we stopped mid-stairs as we heard the plane returning, and saw it roar past through the window. I imagined that I actually saw the pilot's ugly face in the cockpit, which was an impossibility. We stood there shaking briefly, and then made it safely to the shelter. It was the first of my many brushes with death during my lifetime.

After the all-clear siren sounded, we left our shelter, and joined the other kids and neighbours in the street, where people were talking and picking up remains of shells. It was later that day that we heard the awful news of the attack on the Sandhurst School in Catford just a few miles away. It was bombed at lunchtime, and half of the school was destroyed. The school's playground was full of teachers and children running for cover, and the German fighter planes were bombing the area. This cowardly strike killed thirty-eight children and six staff and injured sixty more children between the ages of five and nine.

This was one of Germany's 'Terror Raids' planned to demoralise the population at the time. They would send a few Fokker-Wolf fighter bombers over, escorted by Messerschmitt fighters, to cause disruptions. It was obviously that one of these Messerschmitt fighters involved in the attack on the school, was the one that strafed our street, getting rid of the last of his ammunition — our street being just a few miles from the school. We were glad to hear later that Spitfires had shot him down when he was heading for the coast to return home.

I felt at the time that Gran was my security blanket — my 'shelter from the storm'. Teaching me the best things in life, with love and care. I felt that she believed in me, attempting to teach me to be something special, which went 'against the grain' of the class system that existed with us at that time.

Back With the Family

In early February 1943, Dad was posted back to Chiswick, West London, and the bombing had eased off. He arranged for Mum and the three kids to return to London from Mansfield Woodhouse, and to move in temporarily with his parents in Miall Road, Lower Sydenham. There was room, as my Aunt Alice and my four uncles were now doing their military service out of London. But I was very sad to leave the care of Gran Jeffery and her flat where I had been so happy, I remember crying when I said goodbye to her. However, I did cheer up when I joined brother John and sister Anne again, and saw our little six-month-old sister Judy for the first time.

One weekend Dad returned home briefly, and when he went back to the barracks, he took me with him. On arrival I was introduced to a few of his soldier friends, who showed me their rifles, and demonstrated how they loaded them, which impressed me. I think Dad had taken me away with him to give Mum a break, which was confirmed when we left. We went on to the home of a soldier friend of his, whose family owned a large Victorian house on the River Thames in Maidenhead. I was invited to stay the weekend there and spend time with their three children.

Next evening, we were all taken to the local cinema to see the film *The Wizard Of Oz*, my first cinema experience. It was meant to be a treat but with me being so young, and having never been to a cinema before, it scared the life out of me. I was terrified of those larger-than-life-sized characters — the scarecrow, the tin man, lion and wicked witch, on that big screen — and the sounds were so loud that it hurt my ears. It was all too real for me and I wanted to leave but was unable to. I ended up never being able to enjoy seeing that film ever again. I spent a few more days there and enjoyed playing with the children close to the river, before returning to my family.

For a few weeks after that, Dad's two youngest sisters, Dolly and Bessie, would take me on Saturday mornings from Lower Sydenham to Honor Oak Park. We travelled there by tram — a wonderfully wild, windy, noisy contraption with wooden seats and no windows. There I took my very first piano lessons from an old German or Austrian lady called Miss Oppenheimer for a shilling a lesson. I presumed this was Mum's idea, but it may have been suggested to her by Gran Jeffery. I would practise on the same piano that Dad taught himself on in earlier times, but sadly, my lessons were terminated after a few weeks when money became scarce.

One day I was given the job of taking Grandfather's two accumulator batteries to the shop down the road for recharging. They were for the house radio, that they had on for most of the days and evenings listening to the news and the popular music of the time. I was fascinated to see Dad's three younger sisters grouped around the radio, listening and singing along to all the songs, and swooning over the dance bands and singers they heard. The Glenn Miller and Benny Goodman bands were among the big names at the time, and Frank Sinatra was emerging as a solo singer. There were also some great dance bands in England at the time like Ray Noble and Ambrose, with their wonderful singers Al Bowlly, Sam Brown and Elsie Carlisle. I must have been very impressed at the time, as throughout the rest of my life, whenever I heard any of those pre-war songs, I was warmed with wonderful nostalgic memories of the joy they brought to the house during these very dark and depressing war years.

We soon moved up the road to a house that had become vacant when the family living there evacuated. We settled in comfortably and became friends with the Burton family who lived next door. However, their big son Jimmy used to bully me and hit me all the time and make me cry. I eventually decided to get my revenge somehow. I knew where he walked home from school, and I climbed around the back of the wall beside the corner shop, where I found a piece of a house-brick and waited. He finally appeared, and as he passed below me, I leaned over and dropped my weapon, scoring a direct hit on his head, injuring him. He ran home crying and bleeding, and after that episode he never bullied me again. He did accuse me of doing it, but his parents never really believed him. But I thought that Dad, if he had heard about the incident, would have been very proud of me sticking up for myself, as he would always insist I should.

On my regular walks down the road to Bell Green with Grandfather's batteries, I had seen a small black two-wheel bicycle in the window of the bicycle shop next door, and I wanted it. At this time, I was earning pennies by running little errands for the neighbours to the local shops and I would help the milkman with his deliveries, for another penny or two. Relatives would also give me threepenny or sixpenny pieces when I was taken to see them. I tucked all these away, dreaming of buying that little black bike. I plucked up the courage a little later and went into the shop and talked to the kindly shopkeeper about the bike, and gave him my handful of coins, which he entered into a small black book.

Occasionally Mum and I visited Gran Jeffery, and I would joyfully stay with her for short periods of time. This eased the strain on Mother, who was again having problems coping with us four small children on her own. Once I got used to the short bus ride to Penge, and now being a mature six-year-old, I would happily take the journey alone — something that could never happen these days. I'd board the bus at Bell Green and travel to the Pawleyne Arms in Penge and walk the short distance to Gran's flat and surprise her. Whenever I left to return to Sydenham, Gran would give me a threepenny or silver sixpenny piece, which I would deposit with the man in the bicycle shop.

A few weeks later, having been back in Sydenham for almost four months, I took my usual few coins down to the bicycle shop, where to my astonishment, the shopkeeper informed me that I'd given him enough money, and the little bicycle was now mine. He took it down from the window and presented it to me. I left and proudly pushed the tiny two-wheeler home, not knowing how to ride it. When I arrived with my prized purchase, my mother accused me of stealing it. She promptly smacked me, insisting that I return it to whence it came. In tears I returned to the shop with Mother, where to her astonishment the shop keeper explained the whole thing. Although Mum never said sorry for smacking me, or praised me for my efforts in buying it, I dried my tears and kept my bike. I soon learned how to ride it and spent many happy hours after that cycling up and down the street.

The warm spring weather arrived, after the cold winter, and we were obliged to find a new home, as the previous residents returned from evacuation. Gran Jeffery helped Mother find us a place to live, and we moved into the first-floor flat at 32 Mosslea Road, near Penge East Station. Three families shared the house and the large air raid shelter in the garden, together with the man next door. We had three large rooms, including a kitchen, which at the time was more than sufficient for us. Mum soon made friends with the other two families that shared the house and helped with the chores.

After Easter I was obliged to continue my studies, and I would take the long daily walk to the Melvin Infants School with my four-year-old brother John. We still had to take our gas masks wherever we went. At school, apart from our lessons, and with the air raids continuing on and off, we were being taught fire and air raid drills. We were shown down the stone steps into the safety of the school shelter, and told to lie in the gutters if we were caught on the streets during an air raid, and to never stand up. We were also instructed how to protect ourselves in the safest places in our homes if we couldn't get to a shelter in time. Hiding under staircases was said to be the safest place, and under tables was regarded as a safe refuge if bombs were falling.

We were also taught the basics of not talking loosely to strangers, and saving rags, paper and other disposable items. There were propaganda posters all over the classroom, and I particularly remember the one of the Squander Bug — an ugly beetle that had swastikas all over it. Even at this early age we were also being shown propaganda films — one featuring the anti-personnel weapons that the German planes had begun to drop on London. These included a thing called a 'Butterfly Bomb'. The short film showed a little boy in his garden seeing one lying there, and stooping down to pick it up, it would explode, killing him. These films were very scary to see at our age, but it was necessary to teach us these dangers at the time.

Meanwhile, the Allies had won the final victory over the U-boats in the Atlantic, and the German and Italian armies had surrendered in Tunisia. I would discover in later years that the famous 'dam-buster' raid also took place at this time.

Summer was coming in every way, and during the school holidays, I went fishing with some school friends in someone's garden pond, and we caught some newts. I brought home my three and Mum gave me a large pudding basin, which we sank into the front garden. We filled it with water and a few stones, and put my newts in. Next morning, I went to check on them, but they were gone. I never knew whether they escaped, or if next-door's tabby cat got them.

In August, Dad, who was by now stationed in Winchester in Hampshire, returned home on leave with a dead pheasant that he'd been given by a local farmer. We had never seen one before, and its beautiful feathers fascinated us. We helped Dad and Mum pluck it ready for the oven, and we kept all the best feathers — using them to dress up as Red Indians.

A month later, having heard that Mum was unwell and finding it hard to manage with us kids, Dad requested a forty-eight-hour pass, which his captain refused. Dad deciding to leave anyway, left the camp and hitch-hiked home. Meanwhile the officer had a change of heart and was happy to arrange a pass for Dad but discovered he had already left. When Mum was feeling better after a few days, and Dad was relieved that it was nothing serious, he returned to camp expecting the worst. But on arrival he was sternly warned by the officer, but not punished. One thing my dad had in large doses was guts.

The summer holiday passed by with lovely weather but owing to the occasional air raid we never went far from home. We spent most of the time playing on the street or in our large back garden. We returned to school in early September, and I was doing really well, thanks to my Gran's tuition, that had put me ahead of most of the other kids.

In October over the nine-day period from the 15th to the 24th, sister Judy, brother John and I had our birthdays, but there were no celebrations, and the run up to Christmas also passed by quietly. When January 1944 arrived, the weather got much colder. We began to suffer the occasional air raid, while we were hearing encouraging news that the war was being won on all fronts.

However, the reality of a tough life for a kid in southeast London was rammed home to me at the age of seven. Because of the success I was having with my studies, I was moved up to the Oakfield Road School in Penge, which was fortunately a lot closer to home. Here the classes were made up of forty to fifty pupils in each. Those early days were marked with bad memories that have never left me, but nothing to do with the war. I now had to deal with rough boys and bullies, always spoiling for a fight.

During playtime on that very first day, I was confronted in the outside playground toilet, by a big boy called Jimmy Pearce who asked me if I wanted to get 'bashed up'. Small for my age, I was scared of him and didn't want to fight. But he continued to threaten me, and in panic I turned and swung out, and luckily hit him directly on the nose. Bleeding heavily, he rushed out of the toilets, crying to the teachers. After school he was waiting for me, and I expected the worst, but instead, he was very friendly, and assured me that if I had any trouble in the future, he would defend me. By coincidence in the mid-fifties, we would serve together in the Royal Air Force in Oldenburg, West Germany, and continued our friendship.

In those days before the NHS was formed, we had to go to the clinic that was next door to the school. Each morning after assembly we were each given a spoonful of malt and a small bottle of orange juice and were checked for diseases. There we would have treatments for ringworm and scabies. This involved us stripping naked in the cold room, feeling highly embarrassed. We were then immersed one by one into baths of a sticky liquid. After stepping out, we were not allowed to dry off, but had to put our clothes on as we were — a horrid experience — and sit in class like that for the rest of the day with our clothes stuck to our bodies.

We were also instructed to take letters home to our parents, to get permission for dental check-ups and treatment. Mum agreed, and I felt betrayed. This treatment at the clinic consisted of either pulling teeth or drilling and filling them — neither with anaesthetic. We all screamed in turn, frightening the next batch of waiting victims. I realised later that medical supplies were a rarity at the time, with the military getting priority. These frightening and painful moments were the cause of me dreading dentists throughout my life.

But it is mostly the sounds of wartime that live in my memory, and which caused me to have bad dreams for years after the war. The air raid sirens would wail their warning of a coming air raid and would strike fear in our hearts. Then during the air raids that began again with a vengeance, the trucks with pom-pom guns would drive up and down the local streets, firing shells at the German planes. I remember an air raid one night when we had no time to get to the shelter, and as the bombs fell, Mother threw herself over us children who were all sleeping together in one bed. In that brief moment I realised just how much Mother cared for us.

After these bombing raids, when the all-clear sounded, all of us kids would rush out into the streets and collect our pieces of shrapnel that lay everywhere. They were mostly the fragments of shells from the anti-aircraft guns in our park and the pom-poms that patrolled the main streets, and sometimes these pieces were still warm. We would swap these with each other at school for the best pieces — the favourites being the ones that had screw threads on them.

We heard the true and amusing story one morning from the man next door. He said when our milkman was making his deliveries during one of the air raids, there was an explosion nearby. The milkman was blown up the flight of stairs to the front door of our house, and having delivered our milk bottles successfully, he turned and casually walked back to his cart in the road, completely unharmed.

Doodle-Bug Alley

On 6th June 1944, which would be later referred to as 'D-Day', the invasion of Europe took place with the Allied troops of Britain and America leaving the southern coast of England and storming ashore in Normandy, France. Upon hearing this wonderful news, our mothers were talking about the possibility of a quick end to the war.

However, the celebrations were short-lived, as a week later Germany began its V1 rocket attacks on London. They were soon being referred to by everyone as 'buzz-bombs' or 'doodle-bugs'. Mr. Wheeler, our next-door neighbour shared our shelter during these frequent air raids. One time when the action was a good distance away, he asked me if I wanted to see a doodle-bug, and I readily agreed. I excitedly followed him out into our back garden, where we saw one flying low, with flames spurting from its rear, and emitting that terrible droning sound we were all beginning to dread. I got very nervous and was happy to quickly return to the safety of our shelter.

A few weeks later, on 24th June, the sirens sounded their usual warning and we rushed to the safety of our shelter. The mothers would have a few sandwiches and drinks prepared, not knowing how long we would be imprisoned, and we would try to get as comfortable as possible on the large mattresses that covered the earthen floor in that musky atmosphere. That afternoon we sat silently listening to the menacing drones of the doodle-bugs and watched the mothers praying that they would safely pass over us. Then we heard one getting louder and louder, and I put my hands over my ears trying to deaden the sound and recalling the image of the flying bomb that Mr Wheeler and I had seen a few days earlier.

Suddenly it stopped at its loudest, directly overhead. I was dreading the worst. The mothers threw themselves over us kids, and there was a silence that seemed to last forever. Then suddenly a tremendous explosion shook the ground, and dust and dirt, with leaves and small branches blew violently into the shelter, and we were all coughing and choking, having been covered in debris. But ours was a large shelter, built to accommodate three families, and had a protective side entrance instead of the normal straight doorway and steps down, and this saved us from most of the debris that was blown in, the entrance being side-on to the explosion.

We realised that we were safe, and the mothers, who were hugging us, were crying with relief. When the all-clear sounded, we struggled out of the shelter and emerged into a very different back garden, with fragments of bushes and trees, and debris everywhere. Turning to go back into our home, we saw that the backs of all of the houses on our side were damaged, with the huge French windows on the first floors, laying in everyone's back gardens. The flying bomb had glided down and exploded just over the next street, flattening about a dozen houses. Upon re-entering the house, we found that every stitch of furniture had been flung against the walls in the direction of the explosion, rather than away from it. To us this was an extremely odd thing to have happened, and yet there was very little damage done to the furniture.

Mum quickly contacted Dad at his barracks, and he was given five days of what was referred to as 'enemy action leave', and he arrived home to sort out our immediate problems. He got in touch with the Crowder family in Mansfield again, who informed him that the number 117 Sherwood Street house, a little farther up the road from them, had become vacant and was available to us.

Dad immediately arranged for mother and my younger brother and sisters to be evacuated back to the safety of Mansfield Woodhouse again, where they would occupy the vacant house. It was then agreed that I should return to live with Gran Jeffery again, and the news thrilled me. However, I was a little sad to realised that I would be separated from the family yet again. Before we parted next day,

Mum and Dad sat me down and told me to be a strong little soldier, and I held back tears as I said farewell to them all yet again.

I returned to the comfort of Gran Jeffery's cosy little flat and went back to school as summer term was ending. But I was one of the very few pupils that were attending school at the time. It was a period when history was being made and us kids would have these vital events etched into our minds, never to be forgotten. Apart from the shortages of food, our losses and separations from family and friends were just a few of the sacrifices we endured at this time. The camaraderie within the community was extraordinary, with everyone banding together to a common goal. There wasn't a home in our street that wasn't open to adults and children to walk into during those harrowing times. Everyone helped each other by sharing food, swapping clothing, and assisted each other with any problems.

Hitler had been trying to destroy the British spirit and morale for over four years, but by now it had never been stronger. Even I, as a young seven-year-old, was fully aware of this, and it was brought home to me with a special event. Everybody including the grown-ups and us children from the local schools, were asked to assemble on the pavements of Maple Road, Penge, where the market sometimes stood. There we were all shocked to see our wonderful Prime Minister Winston Churchill drive up in a convoy of open cars and stop just twenty feet away from me. He waved to us, smoking his big cigar, He gave a short stirring speech of encouragement and made his 'V For Victory' sign, and we proudly cheered him as he left and the convoy drove on.

By now Paris, and a week later Brussels, had both been liberated by the Allied armies, which was great news. But we were still suffering heavily from the doodle-bug attacks that seemed to have increased. We would learn later that English Intelligence had passed false information back to Germany, saying the doodle-bugs were over-shooting London. The Germans then reduced the fuel supply which shortened their travelling distances, causing them to now fall mostly on south London, instead of in the city.

Within days, another doodle-bug flew over, missing us by a few hundred yards, and exploded in Laurel Grove. After the all-clear, us kids in our street went round the corner to look at the damage. There we found a large area on each side of the road flattened, where about a dozen houses had earlier stood. We rummaged through the rubble, excitedly picking up the odd toy or book until we were chased away by the air raid wardens, taunting them as we left.

Sadly, the hard truth hit us like a hammer at school the next morning. Our teacher pointed to the two empty desks in our classroom, informing us that our two girl school friends had been killed in that Laurel Grove attack. The bomb that had narrowly missed us, had made a direct hit on their air raid shelter and there were no survivors. The class spent a few moments in silence, and I felt very guilty of scavenging their belongings from their homes, which were now just a pile of rubble.

School continued for about another week, and by now small bottles of fresh milk and a nasty-tasting spoonful of cod liver oil had replaced the malt we'd grown to like and the orange juice we were given at the clinic each morning. This was vital for the health of us children, because at home we were confined to sparse rations of tins of dried milk, dried eggs and dried potatoes. Our standard meat was tins of spam and corned beef. Rabbit was rather special, thanks to Grandad being given the occasional one for doing his slaughtering. Chicken or duck was a really special treat, only to be enjoyed over the next half-dozen years at Christmas. Gran continued to make cheap simple foods that would fill us up. These included milk puddings of rice, macaroni and semolina, bread and butter puddings, and spotty dick (a suet pudding with currants). Treacle puddings and tarts were my special favourites, together with her fabulous bread puddings.

As school closed for the summer holidays, the bombing worsened. Germany began attacks with the new V2 rocket. As opposed to the doodle-bugs, that were still falling, that we could always hear approaching, the V2 was silent. They were launched and would climb more than a hundred miles up into the atmosphere, where they would run out of fuel. They would then plunge to the Earth gaining speed, and exploding on impact, causing much loss of life and damage. Luckily for us, the only one of these that fell near our home, landed on the north-east side of the Crystal Palace grounds causing no real damage. These grounds, that would later be turned into a huge sporting facility, were at the time being used to store military weapons and large quantities of ammunition.

In recent years I found a booklet showing the damage to the Crystal Palace, Penge and Anerley areas during the war. There was a diagram detailing the bombs that fell in that roughly one-mile radius of Gran's home. It showed the one V2 rocket I just mentioned, sixteen V1 rockets (doodle-bugs) and thirty-eight incendiary bombs. It was no wonder the area was called doodle-bug alley, with us spending half of the time living in the shelters during those harrowing years, listening to the dreaded wail of the air raid sirens, the drone of the German planes, and the sounds of the anti-aircraft guns firing from our streets, and the parks nearby.

Happy Times with Gran Jeffery

Looking back, I can only be thankful for this forced separation from my family that the war imposed on me. It was a blessing in disguise, to return again to the love of my grandma. She was my role model and I listened to every word of her teachings and wisdom. During those months she read to me many of the classics including *Gulliver's Travels*, *Robinson Crusoe*, *Treasure Island*, and *The Wind in the Willows* — which is still my favourite children's book.

One day she presented me with a small blank scrapbook and taught me how to cut out interesting things from her occasional newspapers or magazines. She showed me how to make the sticky paste from flour, to stick my selections in with. She also got me to write small diary entries beside them — which I would continue from that day on, well into my early teens.

When Gran insisted that my hair was too long, I would have to walk around the corner to Maple Road to have my hair cut by Mister Wist the barber. He would crop my hair short with clippers and scissors, and I would be aware of the grown men waiting for a shave with his cut-throat razor. There were colourful metal signs on his walls that I fondly remember looking at while he clipped away. One advertised the sale of cigarettes at '2 pennies for 10', while another advertised Swan Vestas Matches. I disliked having my hair cut even then, as the cloth he put round me was already covered in other people's hair cuttings that would go down my shirt and make me itch for the rest of the week.

If I reluctantly agreed to have my hair cut, Gran would give me a halfpenny, and when I was suitably shorn of my hair, I would go a few doors away to the small Tesco shop. There I would buy a small bag of broken biscuits — something that was always available to us at the time. Back home with my little treat I would search through the fragments and if my luck was in, I would discover the occasional piece with chocolate on one side — a real luxury.

Gran began to buy me a sixpenny stamp every week, that I would stick it into a little stamp book she gave me. When I had filled my first book, worth ten shillings (fifty pence), she would put it away safely and start a new one for me. She continued to do this throughout the years I lived with her. She finally opened a Post Office savings account for me, and the books of savings stamps were transferred into it. This started my habit of collecting postage stamps, that has continued throughout my life, and together with this hobby I now have a large ongoing collection of First Day Covers.

She continued to teach me a multitude of subjects that included the basics of maths, history, geography and literature — over and above what I was already learning at school. But she always insisted on one stipulation. Everything had to be kept in order, and this rule has followed me throughout my life, while people around me were untidy and happy to live in chaos. There's not a day goes by when working on the archiving of my catalogues and collections, without me gratefully thanking her for educating me.

Gran had a bookshelf at the flat that contained some very interesting books. I discovered one on the history of the Olympics, another about the Great Barrier Reef in Australia that I loved to read, and a complete collection of seven volumes of *South Africa and the Transvaal War* — a duplicate set of which I was able to buy in recent years and once again enjoy the amazing illustrations, that took my mind back to those special moments I shared with Gran.

The air raids continued throughout those summer holidays, and Oakfield School was partly damaged by a bomb. On our return to school in September 1944, we were transferred to Anerley School, while our school was being repaired. Behind our new school there was a farm that bred ducks and geese.

and us boys would nick a few eggs and take them home to supplement our meagre rations.

When the bombing eased off, we spent more time living as normally as possible, and I returned to Oakfield School. The boys there had a great hobby of skating cigarette cards up against a wall, and when one landed on the other boy's cards, they were won. I myself would fall foul to this game. Gran had earlier shown me her little books of cigarette cards that she had collected over the years. When I asked, she foolishly let me remove them, and take these little treasures to school, where I lost them all playing against the older, more experienced boys. I have however, over the years made myself a large collection of cigarette cards — some valuable ones dating back to the early 1900s — somehow making up for the ones I lost at school so many years ago.

Mum's younger sister, my Aunt Dorothy, now nineteen, was at this time going out with American or Canadian servicemen. I remember them coming to the house and giving me my very first chewing gum and the odd 'rare' chocolate bar. They would take my aunt off to dances in the Purley and Croydon ballrooms, where they would dance to the big bands. I later learned that this was happening throughout the many towns in England, helping to keep the morale high. Silk stockings became all the rage, and the young girls were being gifted them from the visiting soldiers.

One Saturday evening, Aunt Dorothy took me to a large dance hall near Croydon — probably baby-sitting me — or to keep her out of trouble. While everyone was up dancing the jitterbug (the early form of jiving), I would sit at the table with a glass of lemonade and watch the goings on. They were dancing to a big band, and I was fascinated by the sound and the amazing energy I experienced in the room. It was a wonderful moment, of me realizing the power that live music could bring. It took me back to when I would watch my young aunts in Sydenham thrilling to the music on Grandad's radio. There was so much happiness and joy in that dance hall and sitting there I dreamed about being in a real dance band when I grew up. But to me at the time it was pure fantasy, and I thought it could never happen in real life.

The Family Return to London

By early September 1944 the effects of the war were still with us, with the continuation of the heavy rationing of foodstuffs and the separation of families. Even though the bombing raids had stopped that late spring, the V1 and V2 rockets were still falling regularly.

However, my school friend John Russell and his family, who lived up the road from Gran, moved to Woodbine Grove. Gran Jeffery heard of this and made enquiries and secured the house for my family. A week later Mum and the children returned from Mansfield Woodhouse and moved into the now vacant house at 60 Blenheim Road, Penge. I re-joined them, and Dad also arrived for ten days' privileged leave to help us get settled in.

Being reunited with the family had its advantages, but also disadvantages. While living in Mansfield they had created a routine of their own, which I was expected to 'fall in line' with. This caused me to feel rather like an outsider or a stranger. I wasn't the same boy they had said goodbye to, after we were bombed out by the doodle-bug. I was again very unhappy to leave the comfort and love of Gran, and the wonderful wisdom she was passing on to me daily.

Here we had the use of a whole house compared with Gran Jeffery's flat down the road. The front door went straight onto the pavement and there was a small wall, just two feet high, that stood between the houses and the pavement, behind which people would park their bicycles, ladders, and other items. The ground floor of the house was made up of a front room, a small middle room, and a kitchen and scullery. Upstairs were the two main bedrooms — with a smaller one and a box room above the downstairs kitchen and scullery. Mum, and Dad (when he was home), had the front bedroom, while brother John and I shared a double bed in the middle room. My sisters Anne and Judy shared a small bed in the little back bedroom.

We still had gas lighting, as electricity wouldn't be installed for another half-dozen years. The house was always cold, with the stove range in the kitchen, that burned coal, being the only heating in the entire house. The scullery — the small area between the kitchen and the back door, contained a gas cooker, where we boiled the kettle and saucepans of water. There was also a brick copper.

This had a small fire underneath that would heat the water in the large metal bowl above, where Mum washed our clothes. It was protected by a wooden lid on the top with a handle.

In the corner of the scullery was an old mangle that Mum would wind the wet clothes through before hanging them on the washing line in the garden. The clothes were attached with carved wooden pegs Mum bought from an old gypsy lady who would come by occasionally selling her wares. If the weather was bad the washing would be hung on lines in the kitchen and scullery to dry. Mum would then iron things with an old heavy iron with a wood handle that she heated on the kitchen stove range.

There was also a sink that I recall was always full of dirty crockery, and a cold water tap that was our only means of cleaning ourselves. The dish cloth there doubled as a face flannel, and we dried with the single small thin towel hanging on the back door. We shared a toothbrush when there was one, but we never had toothpaste and cleaned our teeth with salt, so we would all suffer with bad teeth.

We didn't have chamber pots under our beds like at Gran's flat. This made it necessary for us to get up in the night and make our way into the garden to the toilet attached to the back of the house. I used to be really scared of the dark shadows and strange sounds I would hear between leaving the house and entering the toilet. My heart would pound with fear as I stood or sat there, with the seat always uncomfortably cold. Sometimes I would hear cats fighting or the occasional howl of a dog nearby that made me finish as fast as I could. Then I'd get ready, quietly hold the chain, and as I pulled it and the toilet began to flush noisily, I'd rush like mad into the house to safety and back to bed.

These fears were added to when our new neighbours, Jim Maddocks and his family, moved in next door. Jim was a big strong man, quite strange and a little simple, but completely harmless. He would stand in his back garden in the late evenings and at night, smoking his home-made cigarettes in the shadows. Then every time one of us (male or female) went out to use the toilet, we would be greeted from the shadows with the words 'Wotcha Fred', even though there was obviously no Fred in the family. After our early fears of him standing in the dark had passed, it became a bit of a joke, and made our nightly excursion to the toilet a little more bearable.

On Saturday nights Mum would stoke up the old stone copper in the scullery, and also boil water in pots and pans. I would take down the large zinc metal bath from the back garden wall and bring it into the middle of the kitchen. We would fill it with the hot water, and starting with the youngest, we would have our weekly bath, and wash our bodies and hair with a large bar of Lysol soap. We'd then dry ourselves with that one thin worn towel on the back of the door and go off to bed in turn. I was the oldest and would end up last in the semi-cold mucky bath water, getting out probably dirtier than when I went in. I would try to dry myself off with that five-times-used wet towel. Then before bed I'd have the unenviable task of emptying the bath water into the outside drain and hang it back on the wall.

New clothes were a rarity and we handed down everything that we possibly could. Others we shared with our kindly neighbours. We wore one pair of socks each week, by which time they would stand up on their own beside our beds at night. In the mornings we would beat them on the bedposts until they softened up enough to wear. This was a necessary chore — especially in winter.

Mum began to teach me how to darn socks, and she was also teaching us all how to knit and sew. We also learned how to make rugs from canvas and old rags, which we cut into thin strips and threaded through and tied with knots. Mum would sometimes sell these or keep them for our own floors.

There were problems with mice and rats throughout the length of the street. We were given a little terrier dog by a neighbour that we named Sandy, and he would keep them at bay around our house and back garden. This necessitated Mum buying him dog biscuits, and after we experimented a few times, we would steal a few, and chew on them when we were hungry — which was often the case, as food rationing was still in full force, and we were very short of money.

After school on most days brother John and I would go to the market in Maple Road and pick up the damaged and rotten fruit and vegetables thrown out by the stall keepers and take them home where Mum would cut out the good bits to supplement our diet. On one occasion, when there was really nothing to eat except a little bread, Mum asked me to go to the bomb site at the top of the road and pick dandelion leaves. When I returned home, we washed them, and had them at tea-time, like lettuce, tucked between slices of bread. They tasted vile, and we never tried them again.

Mother would also send brother John and I up to the Co-op bakery, in Royston Road, to buy a cheap stale loaf for a penny. While the man was getting it, we would tuck a still warm small fresh loaf under our jackets. Being so hungry, we would eat half of it on the way home, getting stomach ache in the process. I'm sure the man knew exactly what was going on but was very compassionate about it. Back home Mum would soak the stale loaf in water and re-bake it in the kitchen stove, and it would come out like new. The families and friends living around us shared the same problems of the tight food rationing, and to us children this soon became the normal way of life.

I would often visit my Gran Jeffery down the road and spend a little time with her and Grandfather, and briefly re-live my special times there, but those moments were short-lived.

In October 1944, my eighth birthday arrived, with no celebrations. But during the school lunch break that day, I went with some friends up to the railway embankment behind the school, where I found a small snake about a foot long. I regarded that as my surprise birthday present, and I kept it for some weeks. It became very tame and would wind itself in and out of my fingers. I carried it in my jacket pocket everywhere I went, including my days at school. With a heavy heart I released it a few weeks later in our back garden, worried that it might die, as I didn't know how to feed it.

If we managed to get hold of the odd coin, we would frequent the shop opposite the school, where we could buy, for a penny, half a dozen small pieces of what was called 'Spanish Wood' to chew. We could also buy a hot baked potato with butter in it for the same price, which was really special at the time. We were an innocent little street gang, who hung out together exploring the local streets now that it was safer to do so.

I must say that it was normal during those wartime years for people to unite to help their fellow man — no questions asked. If anybody in the street was out of work, or ill, or had died, people would go round from house to house and make a collection for the family. As I'd mentioned earlier, people's front doors were always open to their neighbours, nothing was locked, and everybody could walk in and out of each other's houses at any time during the days and evenings.

Us kids would play together on the bombed sites and by now me and my mates had become much more aware of the girls. We would now play kiss-chase on these open areas on the way home from school. I fell madly in love with my pretty classmate Marjorie Baker, whose garden backed onto our own. After school we would go to the Penge Recreation Park, and chat to the soldiers who manned the barrage balloon and the anti-aircraft gun and post there. We would then sit on the grass and she would lovingly comb my hair for hours. I learned years later that she married a local man, but sadly died a short time later.

Dad arrived home on a weekend leave in mid-November and we had one of our few family photos taken in a local studio. By then I had realised that Dad never acknowledged our birthdays in any way, and Christmas presents from him were also few and far between. He seemed to avoid them on purpose, and this attitude had continued for many years and was most certainly a result of his Dickensian, poverty-stricken upbringing, and his difficulty in showing any affectionate love or emotion.

The most attention I got from him when he was home on leave, was at the dinner table. We were not allowed to talk at meals, and when one of us misbehaved and made me laugh, I, being next to him on his right side, would get a slap around the head. I think being away from us so much and not being there to see us as growing up, seemed to alter him. He now felt more distant to me than I remembered.

In mid-December, the great American bandleader Glen Miller, who was in command of the American Army Band at the time, flew to France for their next concert to the troops. He disappeared while crossing the English Channel by plane in bad weather and was never heard of again. He was just forty years old, and I recall everybody around me at the time commenting on this sad event.

With the approach of Christmas, we were taught at school to make huge, long stretches of paper chains from coloured paper and glue to decorate the school classrooms before the end of term. Christmas itself arrived with a great party at our house, that Mum and my Aunt Dorothy organised, with lots of Canadian servicemen and some of our relatives from Sydenham in attendance. We had a great time singing songs and playing games, and the soldiers brought us tinned foods, chocolate and chewing gum. Then, after the celebrations, us kids were all bundled into one big bed with a few cousins, some at the top and others at the bottom. We were laid out like a tin of sardines — and sometimes it smelt like it, trying to sleep with little sweaty feet in your face.

As 1945 arrived, we were suffering with another hard winter. Our bedroom was so cold that the ice would form on the inside of the window in beautiful patterns. We had just the one blanket, that was added to with whatever coats we could find. Brother John and I would try to think of any reason not to get out of bed and step onto that icy cold linoleum. We then had to face the nightmare of having to put on our freezing cold clothes and socks. But once dressed we would carefully walk down the staircase and into the kitchen, where we warmed ourselves beside the hot stove — taking turns sharing the best positions with our younger sisters. Breakfast was usually just bread and dripping, or sometimes jam, and then it was off to school in that bitterly cold windy weather.

The war was progressing favourably with Warsaw in Poland being liberated by the Allied armies, and the bombing of German cities increasing daily, with Dresden being decimated a few weeks later. The Allies were winning the war on all fronts and crossed the River Rhine in late March. A week later, the doodle-bug attacks on England ended, and our air raids were finally over.

On 28th April, the Italian dictator Benito Mussolini attempted to escape to Switzerland, but was captured by partisans near Lake Como and was executed. Two days later Adolph Hitler and his newly married wife Eva Braun committed suicide by taking cyanide poison in his bunker in Berlin, hours before the Russian Army arrived. Their bodies were burned and buried nearby. A few days later the German forces surrendered in Italy, and the rest of the forces in Holland, Germany and Denmark also surrendered unconditionally.

Peacetime

On Tuesday 8th May 1945, World War II finally ended in Europe, and was named 'VE Day'. We had fabulous celebrations with flags and buntings from the windows of every house, and a wonderful party with tables all the way down the centre of the street for the children and the elderly. Meanwhile, the men built an enormous bonfire in the centre of the road, just across from our house, with the wood collected from the bombed houses opposite us. Jim Maddocks, our muscular neighbour, and a few other fathers, ripped out whole staircases, doors and beams to burn. These were added to the bonfire, and the men did a really crazy thing of running up the stairs on one side of the fire, jumping over the flames, and running down the stairs on the other side to safety.

On 2nd June, 1945 my younger brother Paul Edgar was born, although I don't recall ever realising that Mum was pregnant. I do however remember Gran Jeffery often coming to help Mum out with us, together with some of our neighbours.

In August 1945, the Americans dropped the atomic bombs on Hiroshima and Nagasaki, and with Russia absurdly declaring war on Japan, the Japanese emperor signed the unconditional surrender of his country to the Allies. We celebrated what was titled 'VJ Day' with another great street party and a bonfire.

Although the war was over, Father and my uncles and aunt were still doing military service. It continued for some time, but Dad was able to return home more frequently and spent welcome time with the family.

Upon the return to school in early September, my friend David Eastwood and I were so advanced in our lessons — me thanks to my grandma's efforts — that we were moved up an extra year in class. There we were asked by our teacher to help some of the pupils who were struggling during lessons. We would later be the only two boys in our class of fifty-two pupils to pass our Eleven Plus examinations and continue our education at the Beckenham and Penge Grammar School for Boys.

That same month Mum's younger brother, my Uncle Jack, was demobilised. He had served as anti-aircraft crew in the Eighth Army and had travelled throughout North Africa and Italy. He returned with a little Leica camera that he had swapped for his cigarette ration, as he didn't smoke. It was his photographs that gave me the urge to have my own camera one day. A few years later he satisfied my desire by generously giving me my first camera — his old Brownie box camera that he had owned since before the war.

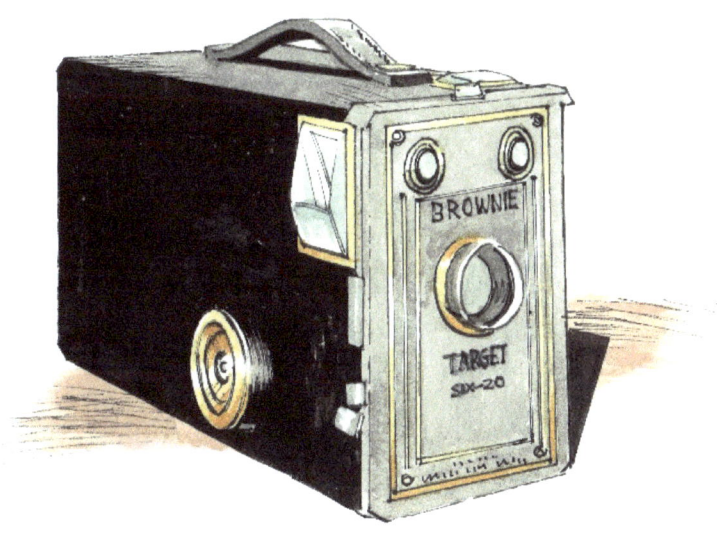

With the war over, and now suffering even more poverty, our street become one of the roughest in southeast London. But Arpley Road round the corner was the worst street in Penge. You didn't go down there unless you really had to, and certainly not alone. Everyone was violent, and some were really wicked; the gangs in these streets were legendary, and some of the boys would later go on to reform schools or do short prison terms. Sometimes Blenheim Road would attack Arpley Road, with bottles and stones, and when we could get them, we would put firework bangers in milk bottles and throw them down the street. Once a boy from our road was hit by an arrow, which stuck in his forehead, causing a lot of mirth as he pulled it out unharmed. It was a miracle that none of us ever got seriously hurt in these battles.

One night in December, sisters Anne and Judy were woken up by noises outside their back bedroom window. They saw two guys in the back garden a couple of doors away trying to break into a safe they had obviously stolen. There were crooks all around us, and even though we were always cold and hungry, we tried to grow up as honest and respectable as possible in these harrowing times.

When Jim Maddocks and his family moved away, my father's eldest brother Alfred Perks, who nobody in the family liked, moved in next door with his girlfriend Kitty Wells. They had two sons but remained unmarried. Kenny was the eldest son and was nicknamed 'Bulldog' because he looked like one and was just as fierce. One day, he started to bully my little sister Judy while she was playing on the bombsite opposite our house, and she picked up a brick fragment and threw it at him in retaliation. It hit him and cut his face. His mother Kitty started screaming about it to our mum over the back garden fence, and I saw for the first time just how protective and brave Mum was. I watched her grab a broom and use it to pole-vault over the low fence and chase Kitty into her house. They never bothered us again and moved away soon afterwards.

Christmas arrived and we were given a gift to share between us. It was our very first *Rupert Annual*, and from then on it became our usual shared Christmas present. Years later I built up a complete set of *Rupert Annuals* from the very first one that was printed in my birth year of 1936 to the present day.

Next day we had a wonderful Christmas party with Dad, who was home on leave. He played the piano, and Gran Perks sang and danced everybody off of their feet, while Grandad entertained us by singing all the wonderful old music hall songs. This is probably the reason why I have such a great fondness for the music hall. But I always wondered why they only invited Dad's family to the celebrations, while Mum's relatives were never mentioned. There was no Gran Jeffery at these happy times, who I was sadly missing.

In February 1946 Dad was briefly posted to Trieste in Italy, but soon returned to England and was demobilised. Back in civilian life he re-joined the family. However, things didn't work out as was expected, and Father and I were continually in conflict over the smallest of things. It became an unbearable situation, and this nine-year-old was more than happy to return to live with Gran Jeffery with her love and care. During this time she ignited the flame of music in me, by enrolling me into the choir at our local church. She then paid for me to commence serious piano lessons, and ended up taking me to the Royal College of Music in London, to pass those first two examinations. This was to become the beginnings of my life in music.

Epilogue 1

It's hard to look back from my position now, to suggest to myself as a child and a young man, how to deal with growing up.

My life improved vastly, from very poor beginnings, growing up in wartime Britain, suffering food rationing until I'd passed the age of sixteen — coincidentally the same year that we had electricity installed in our house in south London for the first time.

I was an insecure, introvert, and a lonely child — small and afraid of the world that I grew up in.

I look back to the day when my grandmother — my surrogate mother — told me — as I now tell you — to try to live my life as is written in that wonderful poem *If* by Rudyard Kipling.

Talking to my younger self, young Bill — be daring young man:

If you see an opportunity, go for it, even when the people around you advise you not to — If you have a gut feeling, take the risk of what your gut is telling you — If people knock you down, get up and try again — If you hope for something that seems unattainable, go for it with all of your might — If you don't buy the ticket you don't win the lottery.

You must step out of that gutter to make something of yourself.

And if you're not successful, try, try, again — and if you want to learn something, practise until you finally succeed — and even when you feel the whole world is against you, stand up and do battle and win the fight and move on.

You may be a little one, but most of the great men throughout history were little ones — think about the likes of Alexander the Great, Julius Caesar, Sir Francis Drake, Leonardo da Vinci, Napoleon, Chopin, Charlie Chaplin and Picasso — and in modern times Peter Sellers, Dustin Hoffman, Ray Charles and footballer Pele, to name a few — the list goes on.

Hard work and perseverance will prepare you for the gift of luck, when it comes your way, so try to live by those last four lines of Kipling's poem, that read:

If you can fill the unforgiving minute
With sixty seconds' worth of distance run
Yours is the Earth and everything that's in it
And — which is more — you'll be a Man, my son!

Bill Wyman

Epilogue 2

Throughout my life God has come and gone, but I often feel that he 'Don't Get Around Much Any more'.

Then, at the most unexpected moments, he will intervene and open a new avenue for me.

I have experienced many 'close calls' in my life, and some extraordinary accidental (or so it seemed), positive results from impossible situations.

He seems to 'come and go' — 'touching bases' on and off — just 'checking in', so it seems. Appearing unexpectedly at the right moments.

I have never seen him — I wouldn't know what to look for.

I've never touched him — although he's touched me at times. I feel him in quiet moments.

We never have a conversation — it's not necessary — he knows. I've never heard him — but I'm sure he's heard me — even in my thoughts.

I have never smelled him — only on a quiet woodland path, in the nature all around me.

Sometimes I'm sure he's there — sometimes I'm sure he's not.

He's my 'gut feeling' when important decisions are to be made. Sometimes I go with them, but sometimes I get diverted and have regrets.

I don't think there's a Heaven and I don't believe in Hell.

He's someone to look up to, and someone to fall back on.

He's the one I can thank for my career, my wife, my family, my everything.

They couldn't have happened by coincidence.

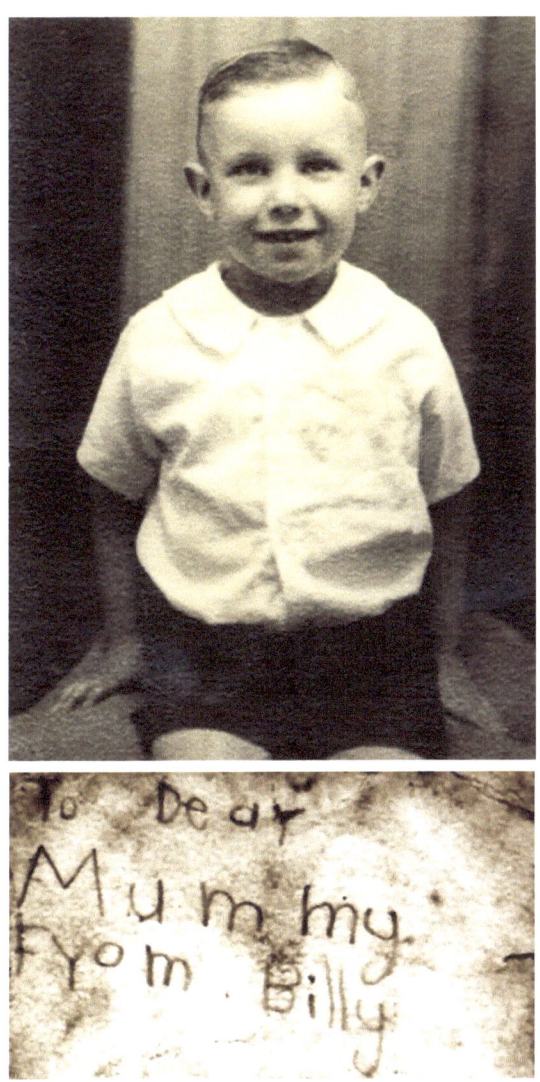

Dated 1st September 1942, this is the first photo ever taken of Bill Wyman (William Perks), age six. Bill and his grandmother sent it to Bill's mother for her birthday the following day. On the back Bill has written 'To Dear Mummy. From Billy'.

www.ingramcontent.com/pod-product-compliance
Lightning Source LLC
Chambersburg PA
CBHW042229090526
44587CB00001B/6